THE LITTLE BOOK OF SUPERSTITIONS

First published in 2024 by OH
An Imprint of HEADLINE PUBLISHING GROUP

2 4 6 8 10 9 7 5 3 1

Disclaimer:

Cataloguing in Publication Data is available from the British Library

ISBN 978-1-80069-632-7

Compiled and written by: David Clayton
Editorial: Victoria Denne
Designed and typeset in Avenir by: Stephen Cary
Project manager: Russell Porter
Production: Marion Storz
Printed and bound in China

MIX
Paper | Supporting
responsible forestry
FSC® C104740
www.fsc.org

Headline's policy is to use papers that are natural, renewable and recyclable products and made from wood grown in well-managed forests and other controlled sources. The logging and manufacturing processes are expected to conform to the environmental regulations of the country of origin.

HEADLINE PUBLISHING GROUP
An Hachette UK Company
Carmelite House, 50 Victoria Embankment, London EC4Y 0DZ

www.headline.co.uk   www.hachette.co.uk

THE LITTLE BOOK OF
SUPERSTITIONS

LUCKY WIT & WISDOM
FOR SUPERSTITIOUS MINDS

(OH)

CONTENTS

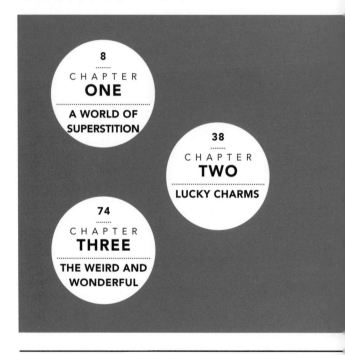

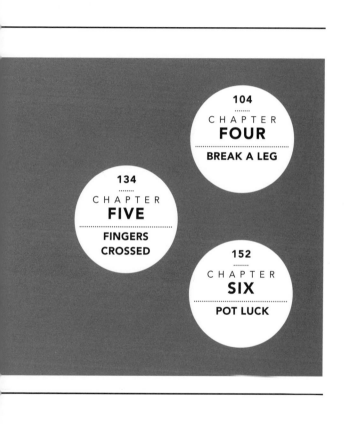

INTRODUCTION

Superstition…

It's incredible how superstitious traits are so commonplace in everyday life.

For more than two thousand years, humankind has remained safe from curses and dark forces thanks to the powerful spheres of influence contained within superstitions. Much more than mere make-believe, superstition is a sacred supernatural belief that several world civilizations have relied on for good fortune. From ancient mantras to lucky numbers, superstitions cover a broad range of tricks, spells, rituals, incantations and old wives' wisdoms to help keep the darkness at bay.

The Little Book of Superstitions is essential reading in these dark days when it feels as if the devil isn't far away.

This tiny tome is a timely guiding light for the one-in-four practitioners of superstitions worldwide, with more than 180 lucky charms to keep close in case of unwanted curses and emergencies.

There are historical facts, legendary stats, iconic quotes, incredible dates in history and, of course, a bright spotlight shone on the very best superstitions from around the world, each one as spellbinding as the next.

CHAPTER
ONE

a WoRLD OF SUPeRSTiTiON

The first stop on our journey into the unknown is a fascinating collection of the world's most famous superstitions and their fortune-favouring meanings – or not, as the case may be...

What exactly is a superstition?

The Open University suggests: "A superstition is a belief that human affairs are influenced not by purposeful behaviour or natural causes, but by magic, chance and divine favour. They usually involve beliefs and practises that attempt to influence events to bring about a good outcome or avoid a bad one."

Now you know!

Touch Wood?

Touching wood to avoid
bad luck is a superstition
borrowed from medieval times
when European churchgoers
would touch the entrance
of wooden churches in the
hope of feeling a divine sense
of connection via Christ's
wooden crucifixion cross.

Superstitious warnings from faraway places...

"Un malheur ne vient jamais seul"

(French)
One misfortune never comes alone.

"En martes ni te cases ni te embarques"

(Spanish)
Don't get married or board a ship on a Tuesday.

"A versare l'olio e il sale, porta male"

(Italian)
Spilling oil and salt brings bad luck.

“

Marilyn Lovell: Naturally, it's 13. Why 13?
Jim Lovell: It comes after 12, hon.

”

Kathleen Quinlan and Tom Hanks
discuss the implications of travelling to space in what is universally believed to be an unluckily numbered craft – from the movie Apollo 13 (1995).

DEISIDAIMONIA

The concept of superstition
began in the 4th century BC as this
Greek word, translated as
"a fear of the gods".

It is probably the origin of the phrase,
"putting the fear of god into them"…

70%

The (incredible) proportion of American students who rely on good-luck charms to help them achieve better grades when it comes to exam performances at college.

If only it were that simple...

Some good-luck charms are newer than others. In recent years, bananas became a symbol of good luck for the national Dominican baseball team – Dominicana – after they started taking bananas out on the field before games as a national symbol.

Bananas are one of the main exports of the Dominican Republic. After adopting the yellow fruit, they went on to win 11 consecutive games at the World Baseball Classic.

Now, Dominicana fans show up wearing banana necklaces to support their country, chanting "Plátano power!"

As you do!

66

Superstition is a part of the very being of humanity; and when we fancy that we are banishing it altogether, it takes refuge in the strangest nooks and corners and then suddenly comes forth again, as soon as it believes itself at all safe.

99

Johann Wolfgang von Goethe
German poet, playwright and novelist
(1749–1832)

"See a penny..."

As the old rhyme goes, "See a penny, pick it up, and all the day you'll have good luck."

A familiar superstition that is recognized around the world, the belief that if you found a penny on the floor, it would bring good fortune as it was a gift from the gods and also protection against evil.

In the USA, the original phrase is believed to have been:

"See a pin and pick it up and all day long you'll have good luck."

This is derived from a pagan ritual in which a pin could be used in a good-luck spell.

66

Superstition is the reservoir of all truths.

99

Charles Baudelaire
French poet (1821–1867)

Some superstitions carry risks.

In Mexico, it's believed that sleeping with scissors under your pillow can stop a bad dream in its tracks.

Scissors are also used by Mexicans to ward off wet weather with the belief that putting a pair of open scissors in the entrance to your home will keep the rain away.

In Portugal, there is one good-luck charm that usurps all others – the **Rooster of Barcelos**. According to legend, this particular rooster played a pivotal role in proving the innocence of a condemned pilgrim who had been sentenced to death by hanging after being accused of theft. The Portuguese keep this symbol of faith and justice in the form of hand-painted porcelain roosters for good luck.

Colour Me Bad

Numbers can be considered lucky or unlucky around the world, but so can colours.

In Russia, yellow flowers are unpopular as they are believed to represent infidelity, separation or even death!

In Japan, the numbers 4, 9, 42 and 49 are what are known as "imikazu" (unlucky numbers).

The number 4 shares its pronunciation with "death," while 42 echoes "to die" in the Japanese language. The pronunciation of the number 9 sounds the same as the words "to suffer".

As for the numbers 4 and 9 together, the pronunciation of 49 is similar to saying, "a struggle from beginning to end".

In Brazil, it is believed that owning a porcelain elephant will bring you good luck – and keeping a pot of rock salt in a corner of your house will keep bad luck at bay.

"

I knew it in my heart.
You can buck the system,
but you can't buck the
dark forces that lie hidden
beneath the surface.
The ones some people
call superstitions.

"

Matt Dillon as Bob
in the acclaimed movie Drugstore Cowboy
(1989)

In the Caribbean, having an itchy palm can mean one of two things – if you have an itchy left palm, it means you will soon owe money.

If (preferably!) you have an itchy right palm, happy days! It means money is coming your way!

In Greece, pomegranates are hung over the front doors of homes throughout the land during the Christmas holidays.

The brightly coloured fruit is a symbol of abundance and good fortune to Greeks. Then, on New Year's Eve – with all the house lights out – the pomegranates are smashed on the doorstep or porch as the clock strikes midnight. The more seeds scattered, the better fortune will be received in the coming year.

In Spain, it is traditional to eat 12 grapes starting at midnight of the new year, eating one grape with each chime of the clock.

The Spanish believe this will ensure a year of good fortune, and this custom has also spread to some Latin American countries.

Wearing red will allegedly enhance this good fortune.

"

WE CANNOT LOOK TO SUPERSTITION IN THIS. THE DEVIL IS PRECISE.

"

Reverend Hale
in Arthur Miller's The Crucible *(1953)*

Brush Strokes?

In South America, be careful not to be around anyone sweeping up with a broom. Brazilians believe that if your feet are swept over by a broom, you will remain single all your life!

However, you can break the curse by immediately spitting on the broom!

80%

The proportion
of high-rise
buildings all over
the world that
lack a 13th floor.

In Japan, it's bad luck to trim your fingernails – or toenails, after dark.

It could lead to premature death!

Consider yourself warned!

"

Fighting against superstition is as hard as fighting against Satan himself.

"

Harry Stubbs as Reverend Norman
in the 1941 movie The Wolf Man

Lucky/Unlucky Playlist

1. "Superstition" – Stevie Wonder

2. "Black Cat" – Janet Jackson

3. "Broken Mirror" – Travis

4. "No.13 Baby" – Pixies

5. "I Should Be So Lucky" –
Kylie Minogue

6. "Black Magic Woman" –
Fleetwood Mac

7. "Knock On Wood" – Eddie Floyd

8. "Spit Three Times" – Neneh Cherry

9. "Born Under A Bad Sign" – Cream

10. "Ain't No Sunshine" – Bill Withers

6

According to English superstition, six is the number of ravens that must remain at the Tower of London at all times, or the Crown of the King will be vulnerable to attack – and most probably defeat!

66

Let me make the superstitions of a nation and I care not who makes its laws or its songs either.

99

Mark Twain
Following the Equator *(1897)*

CHAPTER
TWO

LUCKY CHARMS

Onwards!

We arrive now at the chapter
where lucky numbers and charms
are all that counts.

Luck, fortune tokens and rituals
are renowned throughout the world
and can be traced back thousands
of years across countless cultures,
but no two are the same.

Four-Leaf Clovers

A four-leaf clover is considered to be a lucky find indeed – and you've a 10,000-1 chance of finding one wherever clover grows in abundance.

The superstition can be traced back to Adam and Eve, with Eve allegedly taking a four-leaf clover as a souvenir from the garden of Eden.

Celtic tradition suggests holding one protects you from evil spirits, dangerous fairies and bad luck – finding one to hold is a bigger problem!

66
They're always after me Lucky Charms!
99

Irish hitman Paddy O'Brien
fails to see the connection between his prized jewellery and the popular US breakfast cereal in the 1997 movie Austin Powers.

RABBIT'S FEET

At one time, seeing a rabbit's foot dangling on a bunch of keys was commonplace, and people would carry them for luck without much thought for this good- luck charm.

Of course, it wasn't very lucky for the rabbit it was taken from!

The legend of the rabbit's foot carries with it many caveats to be considered lucky, with some suggesting the poor creature needs to be captured in a cemetery under a full moon on Friday the 13th!

Some believe the rabbit to be a shapeshifting witch, others believe the custom was born out of the rabbit being considered a clever chap and that having its foot would bring good fortune and increased intelligence!

Dreamcatchers

A North American tradition born out of the good-luck symbols used by Native Americans, which are said to bring protection and peace of mind.

Constructed of string, thread, feathers and beads, the dreamcatcher's sole purpose is to prevent nightmares and allow for sweet, positive dreams to be experienced by those sleeping with one close by.

13%

The proportion of American folk who carry a lucky charm at least "sometimes".

7% have one with them every day.

ELEPHANTS

Few would disagree that elephants are beloved mammals, but in Thailand and India they are good-luck symbols that bring abundance, good fortune and strength.

The reverence of this most noble, gentle creature comes from Ganesh, the Hindu god of wisdom and luck, who is depicted as having an elephant's head.

Owning an elephant charm on a bracelet or necklace or even having an ornament in your home are all thought to bring luck.

Alligator Teeth

Some African tribes believe that alligator teeth are particularly lucky – especially when they are gambling!

The symbolic use of alligator teeth continues to this day, with many surfers in the US wearing them for protection – presumably against predators with even sharper teeth: sharks!

BAMBOO

In China, people believe bamboo to be a good-luck symbol.

Linked to feng shui, gifting a bamboo plant as a housewarming present will bring the recipient good luck.

Placing the bamboo in the east corner of a room is believed to enhance the good fortune that the bamboo brings.

66
I don't carry lucky charms, but I believe in those things.
99

Christopher Walken

To many across the world, a lucky charm could be anything: a shirt, a pair of socks, shoes, a tie, a coin, a bracelet or a hat – literally anything that the wearer associates with bringing good fortune.

A 2023 study of 2,000 UK adults
and a further 500 in Ireland revealed
there is more than a hint of truth
in the phrase

"the luck of the Irish".

On average, the survey showed
Emerald Isle folk experience
40 fortunate moments a year,
compared with 37 such moments for
those in the UK (that's nearly
10% fewer).

PYSANKY

The Pysanky is essentially a Ukrainian Easter egg – but very different from the chocolate versions eaten on Easter around the world.

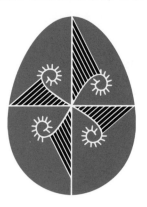

The bringer of abundance and strength, the Pysanky is made using colourful dyes and melted beeswax and are lovingly crafted, intricate masterpieces.

Often associated with Christianity – with the egg seen as a symbol for the resurrection of Christ – the patterns on the egg represent everything from fertility, to strength, prosperity and the Holy Trinity.

Ukrainians also keep their treasured symbol of Easter in their homes long after the celebration has passed.

"

Superstition is to religion what astrology is to astronomy the mad daughter of a wise mother. These daughters have too long dominated the earth.

"

Voltaire

In China, anything red is thought to bring honour, protection and strength. Believed to ward off evil and demons in stories handed down from generation to generation, red is everywhere in Chinese culture.

The tradition of gifting red envelopes during Chinese New Year is believed to have been established in order to protect children and other loved ones.

The Chinese will wear anything red – clothing, jewellery, underwear – for the coming of the New Year in order to attract good fortune.

CARP SCALES

Known to bring good fortune
and abundance.

While many in the West tuck into
turkey on Christmas Day, the traditional
Christmas dinner in many central
European countries – Poland, Austria,
Croatia, the Czech Republic, and
Slovakia (supposedly the source of this
tradition) – is anything but. Their festive
dinner centres around fish – or carp to
be precise.

The scales of the carp are considered good-luck charms and are believed to bring luck for the coming year.

Each gathered member scratches off scales from the carp – one for every member of the family – and when dried, the recipients put them in purses, wallets and pockets and carry them around until they are replaced the following Christmas.

WISHBONES

In the United States and the UK, the wishbone of a chicken or similar is considered lucky – if you win the contest, of course!

Ancient Etruscans believed birds to be mystical, powerful creatures and used their bones to make wishes. The Romans took on this belief, cracking bones for wishes, and this was, in turn, passed on to the British during the days of the Roman Empire.

Subsequently, the tradition made its way to the US via the British, and on Thanksgiving, the turkey wishbone is considered the ultimate symbol of good luck. The rule remains that the person who snaps the larger half of the wishbone gets the wish!

66

I like believing. I believe in all of these Irish myths, like leprechauns. Not the pot of gold, not the Lucky Charms leprechauns. But maybe was there something in the traditional sense? I believe that this stuff came from somewhere other than people's imaginations.

99

Megan Fox

Ladybugs/Ladybirds

Ladybugs are believed to be a lucky charm throughout many different cultures and religions.

Some believe that the number of spots on a ladybug will indicate how many years of good luck you'll have.

THE HAMSA

The Hamsa is a symbol of protection against the evil eye, commonly used in jewellery and wall hangings in the Middle East. It is known in Islam as the "Hand of Fatima", while it is referred to as the "Hand of Miriam" in Judaism.

THE MANEKI-NEKO

If you ever visit **Japan**, have friends from South East Asia or visit restaurants or takeaways connected with the region, you will have seen many maneki-nekos.

While the name might not be familiar, the image of the smiling cat with a waving paw – often in gold – most certainly will be. It is a symbol of welcoming and can often be found at the front of stores, eateries and homes where the maneki-neko beckons you in.

Though there are numerous theories behind the friendly feline, the most persistent is that an elderly woman created a pottery version of her departed cat who instructed her to do so in a dream. It sort of caught on from there!

SCARABS

One of Egyptian folklore's most powerful and cherished symbols for good health and eternal life.

The scarab is essentially the humble dung beetle that the ancient Egyptians associated with Ra, the first pharaoh and the god of the sun.

Ra is said to have methodically moved the sun across the sky in much the same way the dung beetle moves its treasure, earning it the comparison with the powerful and revered deity.

Helpful in life and, according to legend, equally so in the afterlife, where they were buried with ancient Egyptians to ensure eternal life.

 # Horseshoes

For hundreds of years, horseshoes have been considered lucky.

Hung in homes for protection, and provided they are pointing upwards, it is believed they will store good fortune as it passes by.

However, a horseshoe pointing downwards is bad luck, as it allows all the good luck to fall out!

TOP 10

The Irish are considered one of the luckiest of all nationalities on the planet – whether that's true or not is impossible to know, but here are the top 10 lucky charms in Ireland:

1. Lucky numbers
2. Bracelets
3. Coins
4. Rings
5. Four-leaf clovers
6. Ladybugs
7. Socks
8. Horseshoes
9. Rainbows
10. Underwear

THE DALA HORSE

The Dala Horse of Sweden is hugely significant to Swedish culture and identity.

Known in Swedish as "Dalahäst", the dala horse embodies a shared history of man and horse in the Scandinavian landscape that has endured for hundreds of years.

The Dala Horse first appeared in the 17th century as small wooden horses sold in the markets and villages in Dalarna, central Sweden. Often gifted to children, over time the little wooden horse from Dalarna became a treasured object, and it was popular to paint them in bright colours, inspired by the vibrant landscape.

Today, they are considered a symbol of good luck and come in various forms.

The use of keys as lucky charms dates back to the ancient Greeks, who believed keys gave their prayers the power to reach the gods.

Key symbols and charms are popular around the world – keys open doors and offer opportunities and many believe they also represent fortune and freedom.

66

I have no lucky
charm. I am
100 per cent
superstition-free,
and I take nothing
for granted.

99

Jeff Bridges

THE NAZAR

Glaring enviously, the so-called "evil eye" is said to bring misfortune to those inflicted by it and has been a long-held belief in many cultures around the world.

In Turkey, if you have a nazar boncuğu – a blue, eye-shaped, glass-bead amulet – you will be protected. The word "Nazar" literally translates to "eye" or "sight" in Arabic, and many Islamic cultures believe that the "evil eye" is borne by jealousy and envy.

Acorns

English folk have many unusual good-luck charms and the humble acorn is right up there with the best of them.

It is believed that if you find an acorn on the ground, putting it in your pocket will bring good luck and preserve good health.

One of the simplest and most accessible of all lucky charms, perhaps?

CHAPTER
THREE

the WEiRD and WoNDeRFUL

The first stop on our journey into the unknown is a fascinating collection of the world's most famous superstitions – and their fortune-favouring meanings – or not, as the case may be...

What could be nicer than wishing someone happy birthday?

Well, in Russia, it's fine on the day itself, but unlucky if you wish somebody happy birthday in advance.

Some superstitions are a bit odd, but you can see where the idea came from.

In Mexico, placing two mirrors facing each other is thought to opens a portal for the devil – and when you think about it, the reflection of facing mirrors looks infinite.

You have been warned!

25%

The proportion of the UK's population who admit to being actively superstitious.

You might have a hard time eating with them if you're out of practice, but never play with your chopsticks.

In Japan, if you poke your chopsticks down into the food you're eating, they look like the number four, which symbolizes death and resembles a funeral's incense sticks.

Been to a funeral?

Filipinos believe you should never head straight home after attending a funeral as a bad spirit might follow you back.

To confuse the spirit, you should instead pay a visit to shop, eatery or similar before heading home – a practice known as "pagpag".

Do you whistle while you work?

If you do, just don't do it indoors –
at least not in Lithuania, where
it is forbidden because it is believed
to summon demons…

In France, stepping in dog poo is actually considered good luck.*

* If you do it with your left foot. With your right is just plain old bad luck!

To your (not so) good health!

Next time you visit Germany, if you clink your glass and say "Cheers!", make sure you've got anything BUT water in your glass.

If you only have water in your vessel, you are in fact wishing death upon the person you are clinking with!

The Beautiful South?

One of many Japanese superstitions says that you should never sleep with your head pointing north as it will bring bad luck, because that is how Japanese deceased are laid to rest.

In Africa, the same superstition exists but the bad luck only kicks in if you sleep with your head pointing west!

Keep a compass by your bed just in case…

One very common superstition in the UK is not placing new shoes on a table.

In days gone by, people would symbolize the passing of a family member by placing their shoes on the table, so today, to do so with a new pair of shoes is considered bad luck.

CRAP LUCK?

Another common belief – this one originated in Russia – is that if a bird poops on you or something that belongs to you, it will bring you wealth (which you may need to cover the dry-cleaning bill).

Ancient Egyptians believed that hearing or seeing an owl was an imminent portent of bad luck or bad news.

In Italy, an owl in your house means death for a family member. Creepy.

In Iceland, if you decide to knit on your doorstep or outdoors (as you do), you will prolong freezing temperatures.

NEED A TRIM?

In India, legend has it that getting your hair cut on a Tuesday will bring bad luck.

You're kidding?

Rwandan women refuse to eat goat meat in case it promotes facial hair...

In recent years, supermarkets have been selling imperfect fruit and veg as a gimmick to maximize sales of food that might otherwise be brushed aside.

That's unlikely to catch on in Korea, where it is thought that eating fresh produce that is not shaped the way nature intended could see a pregnant woman end up with an ugly baby!

First Footing

In Scotland, it is tradition to perform the age-old custom of "first footing" to welcome the new year.

The "first foot" is the first person to enter a household, usually at midnight on New Year's Day, and is generally a dark-haired person carrying a piece of coal and a pan of ashes.

The origins of this may go back to the Viking invasion of Britain when a visit from a blond-haired person was deemed unlucky. The coal – albeit one piece – is to ensure there will be warmth in the home all year. The ashes represent the remnants of the year just gone.

The Portuguese believe that walking backwards allows the devil to see the direction you're heading.

That's a difficult one to get your head around!

If you happen to be
in the Philippines during a
thunder storm, don't
be surprised to see people
giving anyone wearing red
a wide berth.

The colour is believed to
attract lightning.

RABBITING ON?

In the UK and **the USA**, saying "rabbit, rabbit" or "white rabbit" on the first day of each month is believed to ensure good luck for the month ahead.

LEFT FOOT LAST?

In Spain, entering a room with your left foot is considered bad luck.

Pinch, Punch, First of the Month...

In the USA, it is traditional to give somebody a gentle pinch and a playful punch on the first day of the month.

The practice originates with George Washington, who routinely met Native American tribes on the first of any given month and would offer fruit punch with a pinch of salt added to it – for good luck, of course.

MAN, OH MAN

In Sweden, stepping on a manhole cover will bring bad luck or even a broken heart – but only if the iron cover has an "A" on it…

It's fair to say the Japanese folk have more superstitions than most – and here's another weird and wonderful one. Whenever you pass a graveyard, be sure to hide your thumbs.

The reason? The word "thumb" in Japanese translates to "parent finger", so hiding your thumb is said to protect your parents from death.

Turkish people believe that chewing gum at night is the equivalent of chewing the flesh of the dead – ugh!

In ancient Britain,
women would carry acorns
in their pockets to ensure a
youthful complexion.

Think that's nuts?

Well, have you ever seen an
elderly-looking squirrel?

ONE LAST DROP?

In Cuba, if you utter the words "el ultimo" – indicating this is your last drink – locals believe you are tempting fate and that death will surely follow...

19%

The proportion
of the American people
who believe if they
tell someone the wish
they made, it won't
come true.

CHAPTER
FOUR

BReAK a LeG

Something wicked this way comes... Yes, it's time to turn our minds to curses.

From the Scottish Play to King Tut and the Flying Dutchman to bad-luck signs, this chapter deep-dives into the world where spells, torment and misfortune double toil and trouble in a cauldron of compendium chaos.

Aside from being a long-running horror movie franchise, Friday the 13th is considered the unluckiest day of the calendar according to Western superstition.

When the 13th day of the month falls on a Friday – in the Georgian calendar – people tend to be wary and expect misfortune. Friday the 13th is guaranteed to happen at least once a year but can occur as many as three times in a calendar year.

It is not a universal superstition – Italians believe Friday the 17th is just as bad, if not worse! Mamma mia!

1.72

The number of times Friday the 13th occurs on average per calendar year.

There can never be more than three, as was the case in 2015.

The Curse of the Scottish Play

Ever since the opening night of William Shakespeare's *Macbeth* in 1606, when the actor playing Lady Macbeth tragically died and Shakespeare himself had to step in, it is believed the Scottish Play is cursed, with many historic and recent events to suggest why.

Now, no actor dare mention the name of the play on opening night in case the curse strikes again.

THE FLYING DUTCHMAN

The legendary ghost ship, never able to make port and doomed to sail the seven seas forever, likely emanated from the 17th-century Golden Age of the Dutch East India Company.

Sailors believed the mere sight of this phantom ship was a portent of doom.

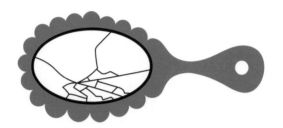

Broken Mirrors

One of the most well-known superstitions is that of the broken mirror.

Ancient Greeks believed that a person's reflection on the surface of a pool of water revealed their soul.

Romans were the first to manufacture mirrors from polished metal surfaces, believing gods could observe souls through them.

Breaking or damaging a mirror was deemed so disrespectful that gods would inflict bad luck on the perpetrator.

At some stage, a seven-year period was attached to the breakage so there was at least an end to the black cloud of misfortune.

THE CURSE OF SUPERMAN

In Hollywood, the curse of playing Superman is the stuff of legend. Numerous misfortunes have occurred to those playing the caped hero, including the suicide of George Reeves and the tragic horse-riding accident of Christopher Reeve.

Many actors who have appeared as characters in the movie franchise have also suffered death, suicide or bizarre accidents, further cementing the notion of a curse.

BLACK CATS

The British have long believed that a black cat crossing your path is a bad omen.

The reason?

The black cat may be on a mission from a witch or be the devil in disguise, and that was, understandably, believed to be unlucky!

Ever witnessed a bird or flock of birds going from left to right?

Ancient Greeks and Romans believed this to be a bad sign for whoever witnessed it...

13

In the UK, many councils instigated legally binding bans on the number 13 for new-build homes, while many developers skip the number when building their estates.

Some 28% of streets in the UK don't have a number 13.

On the Isle of Man in the UK, when locals talk of rats, they refer to them as "longtails", because saying the word "rat" is considered bad luck.

Opening an umbrella while indoors is considered unlucky in the UK – but this is a superstition with some basis.

Invented in the 19th century by Samuel Fox, the early versions were somewhat unpredictable with the spring loaded action and dangerous metal spokes, often causing injury to bystanders and especially when tested in the confines of a home.

Over time, opening an umbrella indoors has become interpreted as bad luck!

In Navajo culture, it is possible to have a truly unfortunate day that could begin by pointing at a rainbow, then throwing rocks into the wind as a coyote crosses your path while an owl flies over your house heading north!

13

There are many birds often associated with bad luck, but none come close to the feisty and busy magpie.

The number of magpies is key to the fortune that will befall those who view this common bird around the world, as this rhyme explains...

One for sorrow,
Two for joy,
Three for a girl,
Four for a boy,
Five for silver,
Six for gold,
Seven for a story, yet to be told.

Crows and ravens are commonplace throughout the world and have generally been regarded by those with a superstitious slant as birds of ill omen.

The birds' unique croak or caw was believed to portend calamity of some kind or another by ancients – a belief that has never quite gone away…

MOONS AND GOOCHERS

In the USA, if a group of people flip coins at the same, should they all land the same side up.

The connotations are as follows: if everyone gets a head, it is known as a "moon". However, if everyone gets a tail, it is known as a "goocher" and is believed to be incredibly bad luck.

"

For he is superstitious
grown of late.
Quite from the main
opinion he held once
Of fantasy, of dreams,
and ceremonies.

"

William Shakespeare,
Julius Caesar

More bad press for crows...

It is considered bad luck if you see a crow in a churchyard. Ancient Greeks – a superstitious lot at the best of times – believed a crow's arrival at a wedding would mean inevitable divorce.

There was also a custom of releasing two crows during the ceremony and if they flew away together, the marriage would be long and happy. If they flew separate ways, the marriage would be short-lived!

The only good luck associated with the poor crow was if you found one dead in the road. Good luck for the finder, bad luck for the crow!

Many actors
refuse to
allow peacock
feathers to be
brought onto
the stage, no
matter whether
they are a prop
or part of a
costume.

Bringing peacock feathers into your home is said to be unlucky, because it can condemn a single female to a life sat on the shelf, apparently.

The superstition is believed to have its roots in the Mediterranean, where evil eye markings are believed to represent the she-devil Lilith, who, it is said, is responsible for the unexplained deaths of children.

Keeping peacock feathers in your home means she is able to wreak her havoc, with the feather's eye as her portal…

39

In Afghanistan, the number 39 is to be avoided at all costs.

Why? It is believed that a sex trafficker lived in Kabul at a house numbered 39 and that their car registration contained the number 39.

It is worth noting that 39 is a multiple of 13…

Wrong number?

A Bulgarian mobile phone company – Mobitel – took the decision to suspend the phone number 0888 888 888 following the untimely deaths of three people within 10 years of who owned it.

26

26 is considered unlucky for numerous reasons. The Gujarat earthquake, which claimed 20,000 lives, occurred on January 26, 2001.

In 2004, the Indian Ocean tsunami was responsible for around 230,000 deaths worldwide, occurring on December 26.

Three terrorist attacks also cost many lives, with attacks in Guwahati (May 26, 2007), Ahmedabad (July 26, 2008) and Mumbai (November 26, 2008).

NELSON

In cricket, the number 111 (or multiples thereof) is believed to be unlucky.

Called "Nelson" after the famous English admiral Horatio Nelson, 111 is said to represent the naval hero's missing body parts – eye, arm and leg.

111 also resembles a wicket without bails – the thing every batter dreads the most because they would be given "out".

FLIGHT 191

After five airline disasters involving an aircraft with the number 191, major US carriers Delta and American Airlines no longer use the number in any of their flights.

The deadliest was American Airlines Flight 191, which crashed at Chicago O'Hare Airport, killing 273 people in 1979.

Delta Airlines Flight 191 crashed at Dallas-Fort Worth Airport in 1985, killing 137 people, and there have been several more incidents for 191 flights that make this the unluckiest of aviation numbers.

I hear you knocking...

Returning to our avian friends, did you know – unlikely as it is – if a woodpecker knocks on your house (presumably anywhere and not just the front door), the persistent pecker is there to foretell a death connected to those living in the home?

Spilling salt is believed to be bad luck – but that impending misfortune can be quickly negated by throwing a pinch over your left shoulder to undo the curse.

"Red sky at night, sailors delight; Red sky in the morning, sailors take warning."

Old sea salts will tell you this saying was taken seriously, with the likelihood that any red tinge in the morning would mean a storm was much more likely.

CHAPTER
FIVE

FINGERS CROSSED

CROSSED

For two
millennia, superstitions have
been relied upon by many famous
and infamous persons of note.
From William Shakespeare to Victoria
Beckham, superstitious people are
abundant around the globe.

This chapter mines the minds of the
curious kind for quotes and quips to
shine a light on their beliefs.

❝

Superstition is born of ignorance and fear and thrives the most when reason is asleep.

❞

Zarathushtra

" I'M NOT SUPERSTITIOUS, BUT I AM A LITTLE STITIOUS. "

Michael Scott,
The Office

"

Fear is the main source of superstition and one of the main sources of cruelty. To conquer fear is the beginning of wisdom.

"

Bertrand Russell

"

I had only one superstition. I made sure to touch all the bases when I hit a home run.

"

Babe Ruth

"

Superstitions are habits rather than beliefs.

"

Marlene Dietrich

"

There is a fifth dimension, beyond that which is known to man. It is a dimension as vast as space and as timeless as infinity. It is the middle ground between light and shadow, between science and superstition.

"

Rod Serling

"

A fool's brain digests
philosophy into folly, science
into superstition and art into
pedantry. Hence University
education.

"

George Bernard Shaw

"

There is no such thing
as an omen. Destiny does
not send us heralds.
She is too wise or too cruel
for that.

"

Oscar Wilde

"

When the human race
has once acquired a
superstition, nothing short
of death is ever likely to
remove it.

"

Mark Twain

66
I don't believe in superstitions. I just do certain things because I'm scared in case something will happen if I don't do them.
99

Michael Owen

66

Through my observations, it became clear that most of society's rules and customs are rooted in fear and superstition!

99

RuPaul

"

No, the menace of the supernatural is that it attacks where modern minds are weakest, where we have abandoned our protective armour of superstition and have no substitute defense.

"

Shirley Jackson

147

"

Blackadder: Actors are very superstitious. On no account mention the word 'Macbeth' this evening, alright?

Baldrick: Why not?

Blackadder: It brings them bad luck, and it makes them very unhappy.

Baldrick: Oh. So you won't be mentioning it either?

Blackadder: No. Well, not very often.

"

Blackadder

66

I'm very superstitious... If I was honest
with you, you would all think I was a
little weird. I don't have any rituals... I'm
one to carry my crystals with me, which
some might think is a little odd... But
I am quite superstitious. I don't walk
underneath ladders and things like that,
and if I see magpies I do the salute-y
thing, which is a little weird but it could
be worse...

99

Victoria Beckham

JINX

There are many superstitions in life, some unlucky, some more fortunate, but what if you are considered something of a jinx?

The name **"Jonah"** was often used by sailors who felt a particular crew member – or passenger – would bring their voyage ill-fortune.

The source of the term comes from the Bible and the prophet Jonah – though details of why are sketchy at best.

Sailors also believed women with red hair were a bad omen on a voyage.

CHAPTER
SIX

POT LUCK

Our final chapter has a bit of everything – some classic good- and bad-luck symbols as well as beliefs, sayings and omens of one sort or another, not to mention the odd superstitious quote here and there...

Ladders

Walking under a ladder is universally considered to be unlucky – but where does that belief actually come from?

More ancient explanations suggest if could be something to do with the Holy Trinity.

A ladder up against a wall creates a sort of triangle, and by walking under the ladder, you effectively walk through a triangle and break the Holy Trinity – an act of blasphemy that could open a portal for the devil.

Another, more realistic theory is that a leaning ladder resembles the gallows that criminals were hung from, which is bad luck for those being hung!

Of course, the most logical reason could simply be that somebody working up a ladder could easy drop a tool, masonry, tin of paint or whatever, as you pass underneath. For the latter reason alone, it's better (and safer) to walk around the ladder rather than under it.

If you unwittingly ever do, walk back under the ladder backwards and then take a different route. Or, walk back under with your fingers crossed until you see a dog. Or make a wish as you pass back under. Or (last one), say "bread and butter" as you pass back under!

Money Spiders

If you're an arachnophobe, this one might not be for you, but of all our eight-legged friends, the money spider is the cutest and most popular.

Some believe allowing it to cross your palm will result in money coming your way, while others believe if a money spider lands on you, it has done so in order to weave you a new set of clothes.

Another way you can monetize your encounter is to throw the poor creature over your left shoulder or dangle it by its thread and circle it around your head three times.

TEA LEAVES

It is considered good luck to accidentally drop loose tea leaves in your home, while scattering tea leaves at the front of your house is believed to ward off evil spirits.

If your tea leaves actually make it to the cup, a strong brew means you may gain a new friend, while a weak brew means you might lose one.

White heather

A sprig of white heather is a good way of wishing someone good fortune and luck.

It is also associated with a belief that the person who receives it will have all their wishes come true and is a popular wedding offering.

The Celts believed that because white heather is rare, like the four-leaf clover, it is lucky to even find it.

Robins

One of the UK's most loved birds, the robin's popularity has never dimmed through the ages.

A symbol of the approaching spring and warmer weather, its association with new beginnings and rebirth means that even the mere sight of one is often uplifting.

The robin is symbolic of supernatural powers, with the old saying "when robins appear, a loved one is near", suggesting the tiny red-breasted bird is a reincarnation of somebody loved but passed.

In Hawaii, locals believe that if you can hear drums beating in the distance, you should make yourself scarce as quickly as possible – or remain in the path of the Nightmarchers, the ghosts of ancient warriors who protect the islands.

Still in Hawaii, don't take any mementos from the beaches back with you, lest you face the wrath of the fire goddess Pele.

Should any lava rock or sand be taken away by tourists, they may be faced with a long-haired women wearing red or an older woman with white hair – Pele, herself, creator of the Hawaiian islands.

And there will be some answering to do!

ALLIGATORS

In Louisiana, USA,

it is believed that if an alligator crawls under your house, you must be extra careful – it could be a warning of someone's impending death.

Possibly yours if you forget the alligator is there!

Crossed fingers is universally seen as a symbol of good luck – the act of crossing one's fingers is believed to pre-date Christianity and represents the powerful symbolism of a cross, with the intersection said to mark the concentration of good spirits that can make a wish come true.

66

All men,
however highly
educated, retain
some superstitious
inklings.

99

H. G. Wells

Tossing a penny into a wishing well or fountain actually has its roots in a much grander act – that of ancient Romans throwing a coin into rivers or the ocean to appease the gods and grant safe passage.

66

If a black cat crosses your path, it signifies that the animal is going somewhere.

99

Groucho Marx

The proportion of Americans who believe there should be a row 13 on an aircraft.

37% believe there should never be a row 13, while 18% believe that if there is a row 13, it should be next to the emergency exit!

Utter the name **"Davy Jones"** to any sailor and you'll almost certainly shiver their timbers!

Davy Jones is the evil spirit of the sea and the leader of the supernatural world under the water.

Davy is said to wait in or around ships in stormy weather, waiting to welcome new sailors to a watery grave.

In Australia, it is considered highly unlucky to light three cigarettes with one match.

The reason?

It was believed during the Gallipoli campaign, where more than 8,000 Australian soldiers were killed, that the lit match would be spotted by a sniper with the first cigarette, targeted with the second and fired upon with the third.

In France, if you find a cat attempting to cross a stream, brook or river, you must leave it to its own devices.

Carrying it over is extremely unlucky and would result in the death of a family member of the carrier.

Staying with bizarre French beliefs, get this one: should a woman iron her husband's underpants while wearing a belt, he will almost certainly develop severe kidney issues. Who knew?!

❝

Superstition is not a
matter of ignorance,
but of intellect that has
not found its way to
certainty.

❞

Thomas Jefferson

40%

The proportion
of building developers
in Hong Kong who
consult a feng shui master
for expert advice on
their projects.

Superstition, like true love, needs time to grow and reflect upon itself.

Stephen King

BABY BELIEFS

Many people believe that more babies are born on or during a full moon, and others think it's bad luck to have a cot in the house before the baby is born, and that the pram should be kept away from your home until the baby is safely in your arms.

Listen to the baby in its mother's tummy - if the heartbeat sounds like a galloping horse, the baby is said to be a girl.

If the heartbeat sounds like a train, it will be a boy!

Few creatures carry the weight of superstition that a hare does.

Believed to be shapeshifters – witches or fairies – capable of snatching children or worse, the poor creature was considered a harbinger of doom for centuries.

Should a fisherman spot a hare on land, they would refuse to set sail, and seafarers in general would not even mention the word "hare".

If a pregnant woman should see a hare in her path, she must stop where she is and make three tears in her petticoats or else her unborn child will be born with a hare-lip.

66

I have tried to keep an open mind, and it is not the ordinary things of life that could close it, but the strange things, the extraordinary things, the things that make one doubt if they be mad or sane.

99

Bram Stoker
Dracula (1897)

A person who
dreams of human or
animal excrement
will come into
money, good luck or
prosperity...
that's some lucky
s**t!

It is a common superstition that crossing on stairs is bad luck.

This could date back to pre-banister days when crossing on stairs could result in somebody falling off and injuring themselves – or worse.

Some people believe
that when a child
is born, the mother
should bury the
umbilical cord near
the front door of the
family home so that
the child can always
find their way home.

Crossing water

Water, being such a necessity for life, is inevitably attached to various superstitions.

One is that by crossing the ocean, the cycle of reincarnation is ended, as the traveller is cut off from the regenerating waters of the Ganges.

These voyages also meant breaking family and social ties.

" Is it really not possible
to touch the gaming
table without being
instantly infected by
superstition? "

Fyodor Dostoyevsky

Many black cat owners try to counteract the supposed jinxed reputation of their moggy by naming them Lucky!

Want to give your baby girl a head start?
According to the magazine *Marie Claire*, these
are the top 5 lucky names for girls...

Iris
meaning "rainbow", which symbolizes luck

Evangeline
"bearer of good news" in Greek

Beatrice
meaning "she who brings happiness;
blessed" in Latin

Jadie
because of the stone transmitting wisdom
and clarity

Kiara
meaning "bright/light" in Italian

17

Surprisingly, 17 is one of the most backed numbers on the roulette table, along with 23, 24 and, of course, 7.

The reason?

17 sits in the centre of the betting table, and many gamblers believe it to be therefore a more likely winning number.

Research suggests 23 and 24 naturally catch the eye when looking at the roulette grid and 7 is popular because of its reputation as a lucky number.

Step on a crack...

Familiar with the saying "step on a crack, break your mother's back"?

Not a pleasant superstition but a popular one in the US in particular. Stepping on a crack is believed to be unlucky as the cracks could be portals to the supernatural and therefore invite entities to harm those closest to you.

If you stumble across a ring of mushrooms in woodland at any stage, you might have just discovered a fairy ring.

A fairy ring is believed to be lucky, a sign of a fairy village below or even a portal to another world.

Powerful stuff.

In Jamaica, dreaming of a nest full of eggs is a good omen, meaning you will acquire great wealth.

Or a lot of eggs.

What better way to end our journey
through the world's many superstitions
than with everybody's favourite –

wishing on a star.

The popular theory is that shooting stars
were believed to be the rising or falling
souls of angels and that if this celestial
rarity was witnessed, it was the perfect
moment to make a wish that would surely
be granted by these heavenly bodies.

Now who wouldn't want to believe that
to be true?